D0753186

Celebrations in My World

Christmas

Crabtree Publishing Company

www.crabtreebooks.com

Crabtree Publishing Company

www.crabtreebooks.com

Author: Molly Aloian
Coordinating editor: Chester Fisher
Series editor: Susan Labella
Project manager: Kavita Lad (Q2AMEDIA)
Art direction: Dibakar Acharjee (Q2AMEDIA)
Cover design: Ranjan Singh (Q2AMEDIA)
Design: Neha Gupta (Q2AMEDIA)
Photo research: Sejal Sehgal Wani (Q2AMEDIA)
Editor: Kelley MacAulay
Copy editor: Adrianna Morganelli
Proofreader: Crystal Sikkens
Project coordinator: Robert Walker
Production coordinator: Katherine Kantor
Font management: Mike Golka
Prepress technicians: Samara Parent, Ken Wright

Photographs:
Cover: BananaStock/Jupiter Images; Title page: Polka Dot
Images/Jupiter Images; P4: Stephen Strathdee/Shutterstock;
P5: Image Source Black/Jupiter Images; P7: Kitch Bain/
Fotolia; P9: Mary Evans Picture Library/Alamy; P11: Mary
Evans Picture Library/Alamy; P13: Image Source Black/
Jupiter Images; P14: Chiyacat/Shutterstock; P15: Image
Source White/Jupiter Images; P17: Brand X Pictures/
Jupiter Images; P18: Image Source Pink/Jupiter Images;
P19: Thinkstock Images/Jupiter Images; P21: Comstock
Images/Jupiter Images; P22: Vadim Volodin/Shutterstock;
P23: AbackPhotography/Istockphoto; P25: Homer W.
Sykes/Alamy; P27: Nozomi Stall/Fotolia; P28: Image
Source Pink/Jupiter Images; P29: BananaStock/Jupiter
Images; P31: Bec Parsons/Getty Images

Library and Archives Canada Cataloguing in Publication

Aloian, Molly
     Christmas / Molly Aloian.

(Celebrations in my world)
Includes index.
ISBN 978-0-7787-4287-6 (bound).--ISBN 978-0-7787-4305-7 (pbk.)

     1. Christmas--Juvenile literature. I. Title. II. Series.

GT4985.5.A46 2008   j394.2663   C2008-903487-2

Library of Congress Cataloging-in-Publication Data

Aloian, Molly.
   Christmas / Molly Aloian.
      p. cm. -- (Celebrations in my world)
   Includes index.
   ISBN-13: 978-0-7787-4305-7 (pbk. : alk. paper)
   ISBN-10: 0-7787-4305-5 (pbk. : alk. paper)
   ISBN-13: 978-0-7787-4287-6 (reinforced library binding : alk. paper)
   ISBN-10: 0-7787-4287-3 (reinforced library binding : alk. paper)
   1. Christmas--Juvenile literature. I. Title. II. Series.

GT4985.5.A46 2009
394.2663--dc22
                                                          2008023586

Crabtree Publishing Company

www.crabtreebooks.com   1-800-387-7650

Published in Canada
Crabtree Publishing
616 Welland Ave.
St. Catharines, ON
L2M 5V6

Published in the United States
Crabtree Publishing
PMB16A
350 Fifth Ave., Suite 3308
New York, NY 10118

Published in the United Kingdom
Crabtree Publishing
White Cross Mills
High Town, Lancaster
LA1 4XS

Published in Australia
Crabtree Publishing
386 Mt. Alexander Rd.
Ascot Vale (Melbourne)
VIC 3032

Contents

What is Christmas?

Christmas is a **Christian** holiday. Christians believe that Jesus Christ is the Son of God. Jesus Christ lived almost two thousand years ago in a city called Nazareth. People believed he could perform miracles. Jesus told people about God.

• People take Christmas trees home and decorate them for Christmas.

DID YOU KNOW?

People celebrate Christmas with family and friends. It is a time of peace, joy, and happiness. It is also a time of fun!

Christians believe Jesus died for the sins of others, was buried, and then rose from the dead. Christmas is the celebration of Jesus' birth. Every year people celebrate Christmas on December 25.

This family is celebrating Christmas together.

Winter Solstice

Long ago, Europeans celebrated winter solstice, or the shortest day of the year, around December 21. They celebrated this day because it meant that the worst of winter was over. People could begin looking forward to longer days and more hours of sunlight. To celebrate winter solstice, people lit large logs, called Yule logs, to make **bonfires**. The end of December was the only time of year when many people had a supply of fresh meat. They feasted, sang, and danced.

DID YOU KNOW?

During winter solstice, there was plenty for people to eat and drink.

People lit bonfires to celebrate having more hours of sunlight.

Saturnalia

Centuries before the birth of Jesus Christ, people celebrated Saturnalia at the end of December. The holiday honored Saturn, the god of agriculture. Saturnalia was a time for fun and amusement. People feasted and gave each other presents. Years later, leaders of the Christian church wanted to celebrate the birth of Jesus Christ. They decided to celebrate his birth also near the end of December. It was close to the time of winter solstice and Saturnalia. They adopted some of the **traditions** of Saturnalia.

DID YOU KNOW?

People know the story of Jesus' birth because it is told in a holy book called the Bible.

Pope Julius I chose December 25 for the celebration. That day was first called the Feast of the **Nativity**. In time, this day became Christmas.

Saturn, the Roman god of agriculture, was concerned with sowing seeds.

The Birth

The story of Jesus' birth is very old. About 2,000 years ago, a woman named Mary lived in Judaea in the Roman Empire. Mary was going to have a baby. She and her husband Joseph walked to an inn in the town of Bethlehem. There was no room at the inn so they stayed in the **stable**. Before Mary gave birth, an angel told her that her child would be the Son of God. Mary gave birth to Jesus in the stable. Shepherds and three wise men visited the newborn baby.

DID YOU KNOW?

People have different traditions for celebrating the birth of Jesus.

The three wise men brought gifts of gold, frankincense, and myrrh. Frankincense and myrrh are sweet-smelling oils.

This painting shows Mary, Joseph, the three wise men, and baby Jesus.

Decorating

People often decorate their homes and towns to celebrate Christmas. The tradition of decorating for Christmas began when Europeans decorated their homes and castles with holly, ivy, and mistletoe during Saturnalia. Today, people often string lights inside and outside their homes a few weeks before Christmas. Some people also place colorful Christmas displays on their lawns. In some cities, office buildings, banks, stores, and other businesses are also decorated with Christmas lights.

DID YOU KNOW?

Some children hang stockings a few weeks before Christmas or on the night before Christmas Day. Small gifts, toys, or fruit are put into the stockings.

At Christmas, many people hang wreaths on doors, hang mistletoe in doorways, buy poinsettia plants, and put up holly. Putting up decorations is one way to spread the Christmas spirit and to share it with others!

This family is putting up Christmas decorations.

Christmas Trees

Christmas trees are popular Christmas decorations. Some people believe that **immigrants** from Germany were the first people to bring with them the tradition of putting real evergreen trees in their homes. They brought trees inside because they believed that the trees would bring good luck to their families. Today, people decorate Christmas trees with ornaments and lights.

• A Christmas tree is a symbol of **eternal** life.

DID YOU KNOW?

A spruce, fir, or pine tree makes a good Christmas tree. These trees are evergreen trees. Evergreen trees stay green all year long.

It is fun to decorate the Christmas tree with friends and family.

Singing Songs

At Christmas, some people walk around their neighborhoods and stop outside homes to sing songs called carols. In the 1500s, people sang carols so that they could dance to the music. Today, people sing Christmas songs to spread holiday cheer and to tell others about the story of Jesus. Some popular Christmas carols include "Silent Night," "Deck the Halls," and "O Come All Ye Faithful." Children often sing carols during school Christmas concerts as part of a choir.

DID YOU KNOW?

Musicians from all over the world play and sing Christmas songs during the Christmas season.

Their families and friends attend the concerts to hear the choir sing. Many people also sing Christmas songs with a choir in church.

These people are singing Christmas carols.

Christmas Treats

During the Christmas season, some people make delicious Christmas treats to serve to guests or to bring to the homes of others. They make Christmas cake and cookies, as well as pies and puddings. Cookies are sometimes shaped and decorated to look like Christmas trees, Christmas stockings, candy canes, stars, and angels.

- Candy canes are treats at Christmas.

DID YOU KNOW?

Long ago, a popular Christmas treat was a porridge-like food mixed with nuts, eggs, and honey. It was called frumenty.

Some people make little gingerbread houses and decorate them with frosting. People may also make chocolate Yule logs. A Yule log is a cake that is shaped like the Yule log that was burned long ago at winter solstice celebrations.

Children have fun making special Christmas treats.

Thinking of Others

One reason people make Christmas treats is to spread Christmas cheer. As Christmas Day approaches, people wish each other "Happy Holidays!" Christmas is a time for people to think of their families and friends, as well as others they do not know. Many people give food or gifts to those who are less fortunate. People **donate** toys for children in needy families. Some people volunteer in soup kitchens where food is handed out to those in need.

DID YOU KNOW?

Some people send special Christmas cards to family and friends. Many of the cards are decorated with beautiful Christmas pictures.

Some people put their Christmas cards on display for everyone to see.

Giving Gifts

Giving and receiving gifts is a popular Christmas tradition. Children often make lists of presents they hope to receive. People also plan what they will make or buy to give to their friends and families. Some people bake cookies and give them to others as gifts.

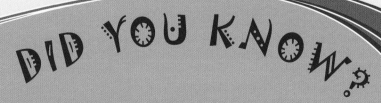

● Christmas wrapping paper can be many different colors.

DID YOU KNOW?

Giving Christmas gifts honors the story of the three wise men that brought Jesus gifts on the day of his birth. People also give gifts to show kindness and appreciation for others.

People wrap Christmas gifts in special Christmas paper and place them under the Christmas tree. Many people give and receive their gifts on Christmas Eve or Christmas Day. Christmas Eve is the night before Christmas Day.

It is fun to give and receive Christmas gifts.

Going to Church

Christmas Eve is a special time for many people. People may go to church on Christmas Eve. Churches usually have candlelight services or midnight masses. At church, people think about the birth of Jesus, pray for peace, and give thanks. Most people also sing Christmas songs when they go to church. Before going to church on Christmas Eve, some people decorate their trees and hang their Christmas stockings.

DID YOU KNOW?

The Church of the Nativity is a church found in Bethlehem, Jerusalem. Many Christians believe that the church is built on the same place where Jesus was born.

Children often take part in
the Christmas mass at church.

Santa Claus

Children go to sleep on Christmas Eve and hope that Santa Claus visits during the night. It is believed that Santa Claus, a jolly, chubby man, travels from the North Pole to bring children gifts. He puts the gifts under the Christmas tree or in the Christmas stockings. Different children have different names for Santa Claus. Some children call him Saint Nicholas. Others call him Kris Kringle or Father Christmas.

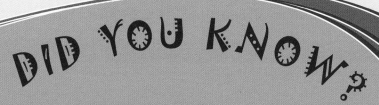

DID YOU KNOW?

*The name "Santa Claus" comes from an old Dutch word for Saint Nicholas. Saint Nicholas was one of the first Christian **bishops**. He was kind to children and generous toward those in need.*

Santa Claus is known as a jolly man in a red suit with a flowing white beard.

27

Christmas Day

Many people go to church on Christmas Day. Families and friends also eat a special dinner together on this day. People cook plenty of food and invite guests to their homes. Different people eat different traditional foods, but many eat turkey, ham, roast pork, potatoes, cranberries, and more.

● Special foods and drinks are enjoyed at Christmas.

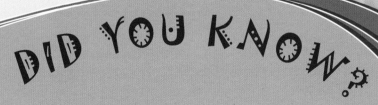

DID YOU KNOW?

Advent comes right before Christmas. It lasts about one month. Some children open a window on an advent calendar each day until Christmas to see a little holiday picture.

Christmas drinks include eggnog and apple cider. Most people are very thankful for all the food they have to eat and share with others. Some people say prayers before eating Christmas dinner. They pray to thank God for all that they have and for those that they love.

Many people look forward to joining their families for Christmas fun and food.

Around the World

In some parts of the United States and Canada, the weather is cold and snowy on Christmas Day. In other parts of the world, such as Australia, Christmas weather is hot and sunny. People can go to the beach and have barbecues for Christmas! People in many countries have different Christmas traditions. Eastern Orthodox Christians give and receive gifts on January 6, which is Epiphany.

DID YOU KNOW?

In Mexico, Spain, and Argentina, children leave out their shoes at Christmas. They hope the three kings, or wise men, will fill the shoes with gifts.

Epiphany is the twelfth and last day of the Christmas season. Epiphany celebrates the day when the three wise men first saw Jesus and gave him gifts.

These children are enjoying a hot and sunny Christmas.

Glossary

bishop A high-ranking member of the Christian church

bonfire A large outdoor fire

Christian One who believes in Jesus Christ as the Son of God

donate To give something to someone in need

eternal Lasting forever

immigrant A person who comes to a country to live

nativity The birth of Jesus

stable A building in which animals are sheltered and fed

traditions Customs or beliefs handed down from one generation to another

Index

Printed in the U.S.A.